INTERMEDIATE LEVEL   1 PIANO, 4 HANDS

2ND EDITION

Christmas Piano D

T0048392

ISBN 978-0-7935-1888-3

HAL•LEONARD®
CORPORATION
7777 W. BLUEMOUND RD. P.O. BOX 13819 MILWAUKEE, WI 53213

contents

4   The Chipmunk Song

8   Frosty the Snow Man

14   Here Comes Santa Claus

22   A Holly Jolly Christmas

30   I Saw Mommy Kissing Santa Claus

34   Jingle-Bell Rock

38   Let It Snow! Let It Snow! Let It Snow!

42   Merry Christmas, Darling

50   Rockin' Around the Christmas Tree

54   Rudolph the Red-Nosed Reindeer

THE CHIPMUNK SONG

SECONDO

Words and Music by
ROSS BAGDASARIAN

THE CHIPMUNK SONG

PRIMO

Words and Music by
ROSS BAGDASARIAN

6

SECONDO

PRIMO

FROSTY THE SNOW MAN

SECONDO

Words and Music by STEVE NELSON
and JACK ROLLINS

FROSTY THE SNOW MAN

PRIMO

Words and Music by STEVE NELSON
and JACK ROLLINS

SECONDO

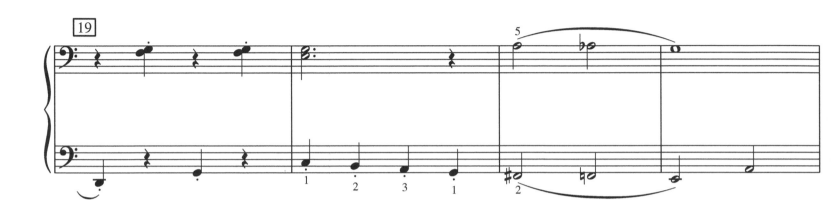

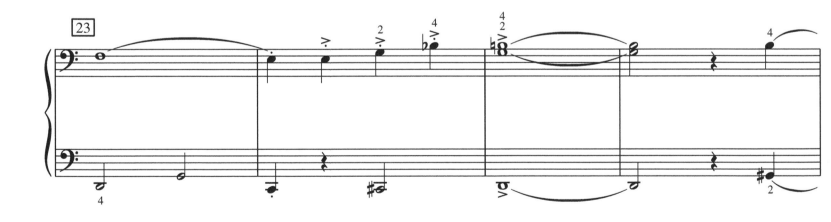

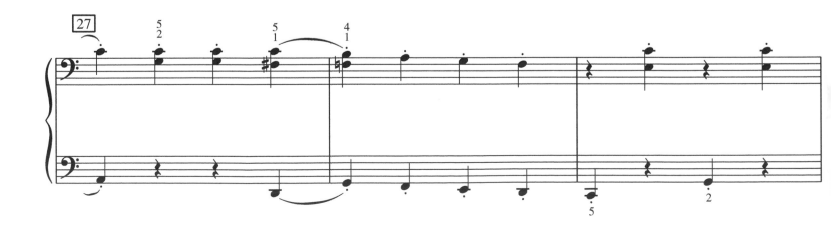

PRIMO

SECONDO

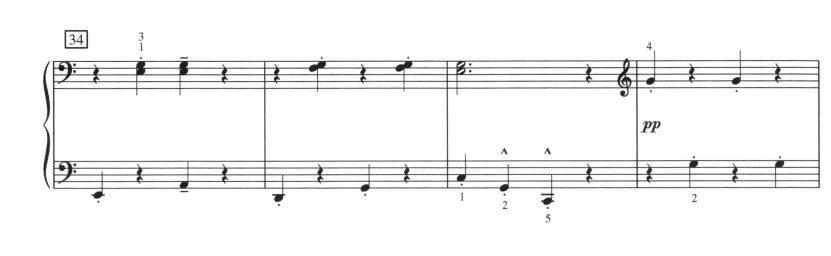

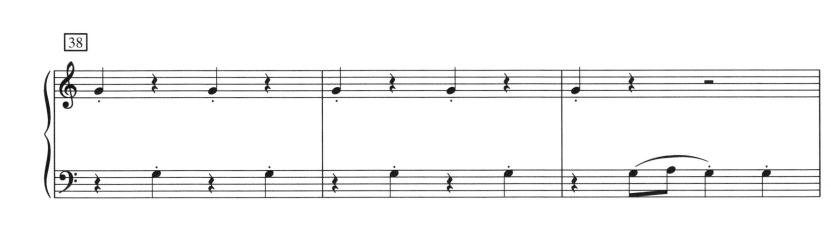

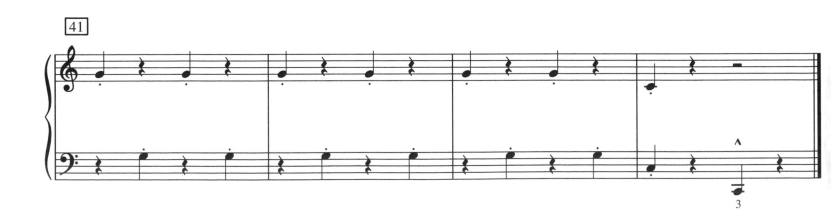

PRIMO

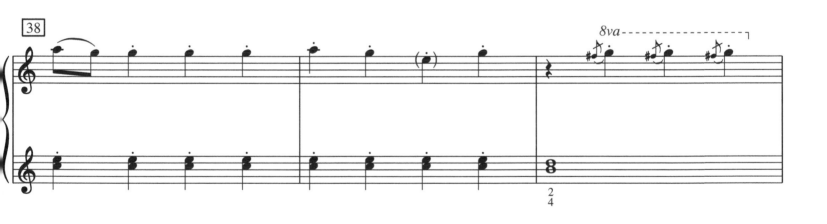

HERE COMES SANTA CLAUS
(Right Down Santa Claus Lane)

SECONDO

Words and Music by GENE AUTRY
and OAKLEY HALDEMAN

With a bounce

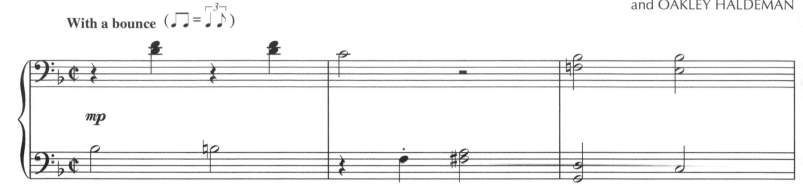

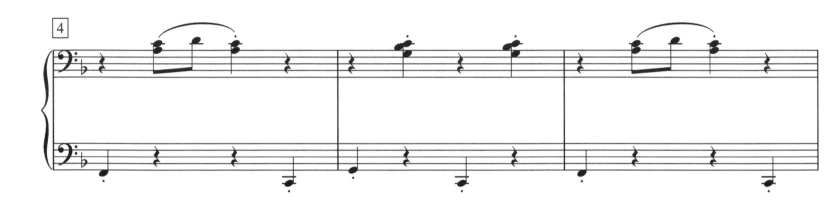

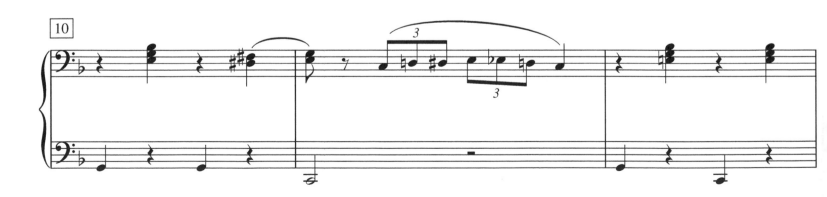

HERE COMES SANTA CLAUS
(Right Down Santa Claus Lane)

PRIMO

Words and Music by GENE AUTRY
and OAKLEY HALDEMAN

SECONDO

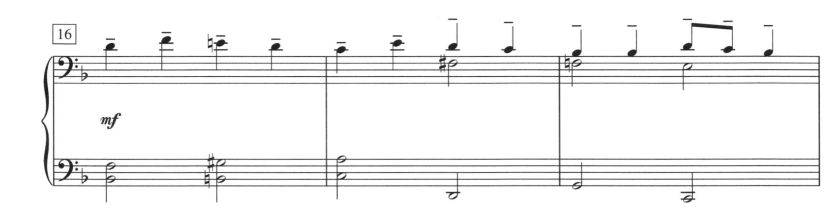

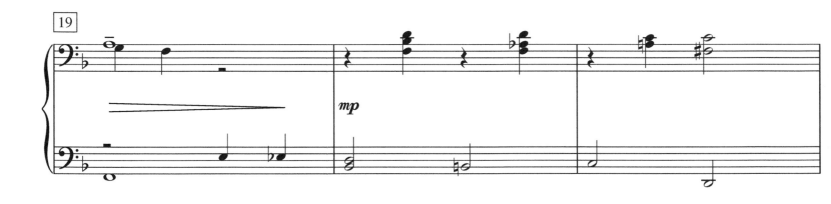

PRIMO

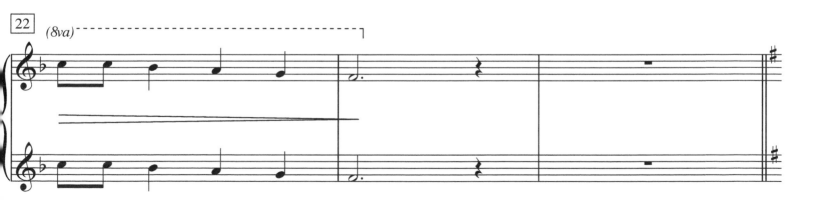

SECONDO

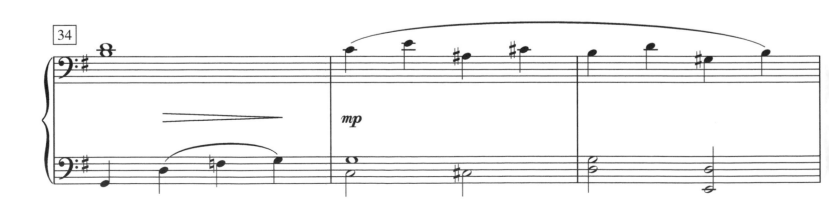

PRIMO

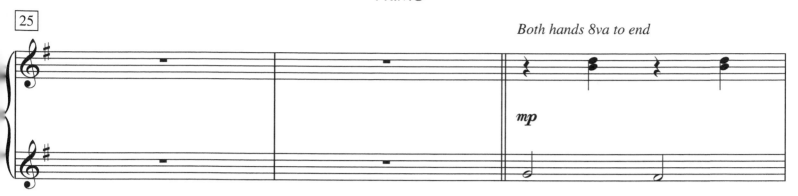

SECONDO

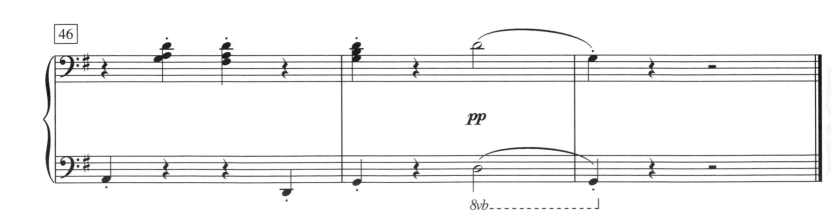

PRIMO

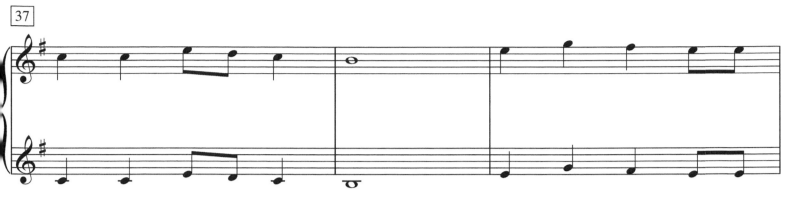

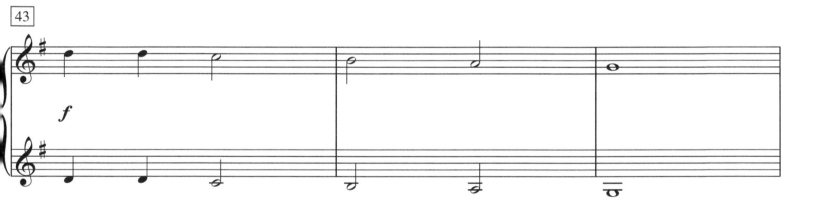

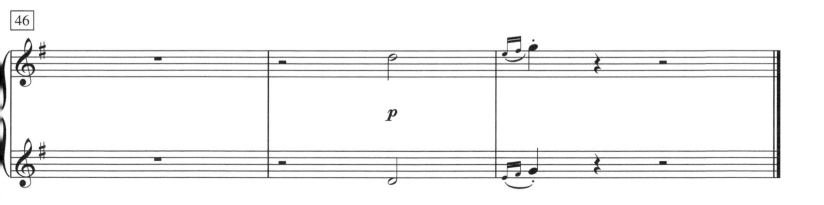

A HOLLY JOLLY CHRISTMAS

SECONDO

Music and Lyrics by
JOHNNY MARKS

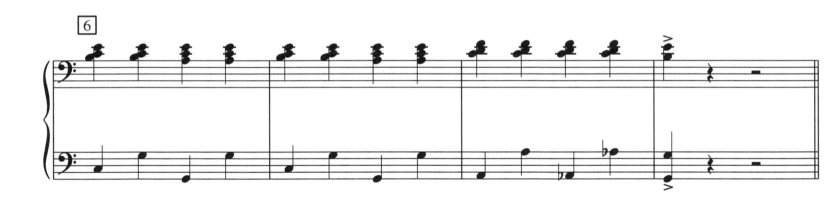

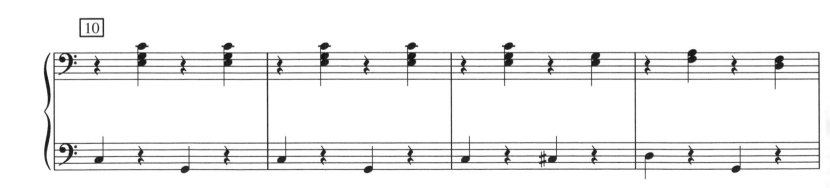

A HOLLY JOLLY CHRISTMAS

PRIMO

Music and Lyrics by
JOHNNY MARKS

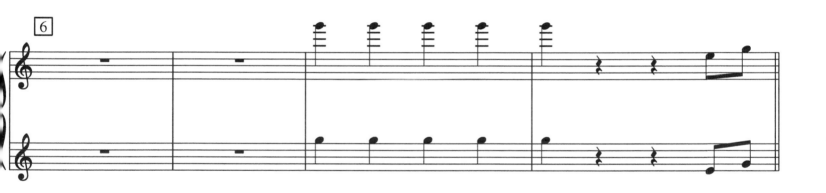

SECONDO

PRIMO

SECONDO

PRIMO

SECONDO

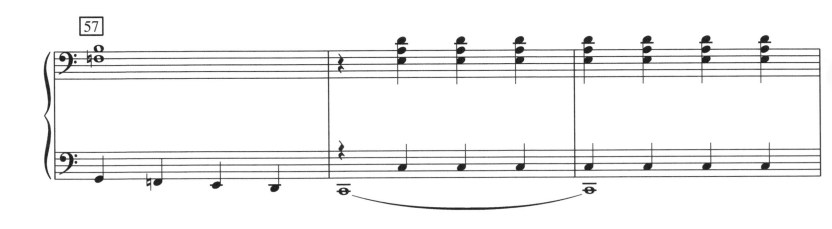

PRIMO

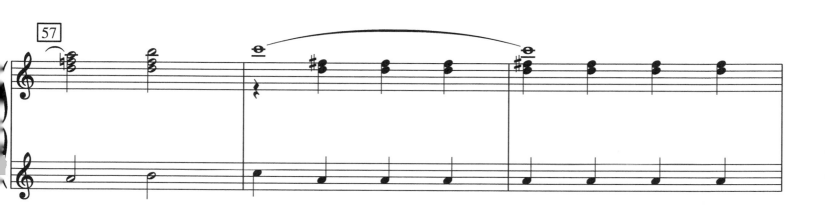

I SAW MOMMY KISSING SANTA CLAUS

SECONDO

Words and Music by
TOMMIE CONNOR

I SAW MOMMY KISSING SANTA CLAUS

PRIMO

Words and Music by
TOMMIE CONNOR

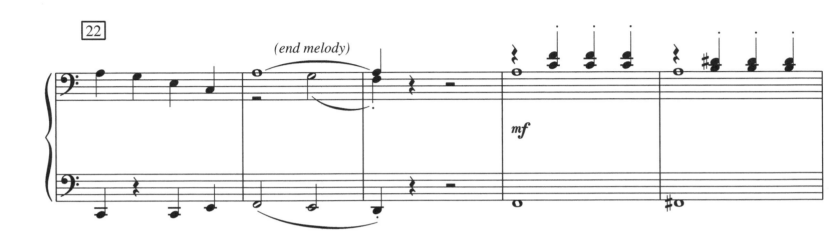

PRIMO

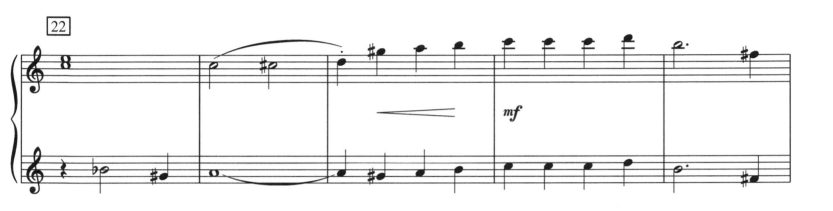

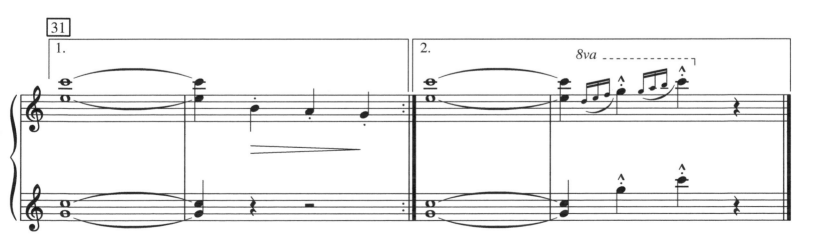

JINGLE-BELL ROCK

SECONDO

Words and Music by JOE BEAL
and JIM BOOTHE

JINGLE-BELL ROCK

PRIMO

Words and Music by JOE BEAL
and JIM BOOTHE

SECONDO

PRIMO

LET IT SNOW! LET IT SNOW! LET IT SNOW!

SECONDO

Words by SAMMY CAHN
Music by JULE STYNE

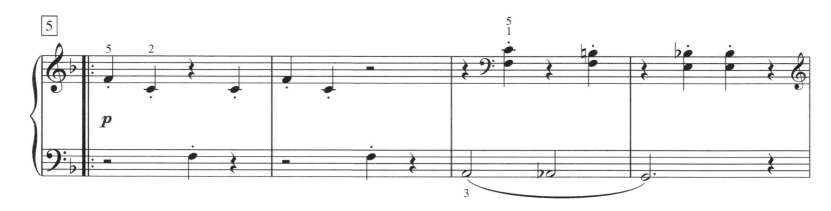

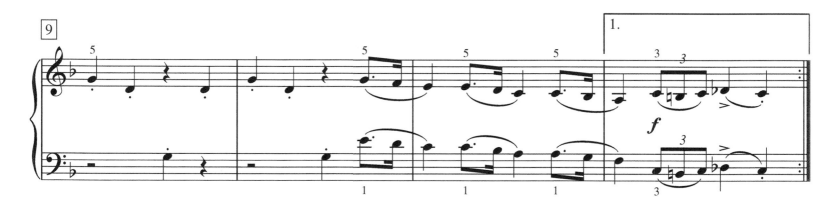

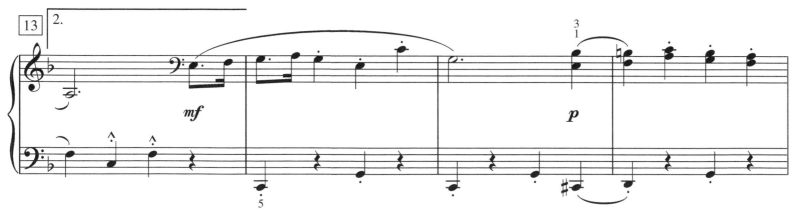

LET IT SNOW! LET IT SNOW! LET IT SNOW!

PRIMO

Words by SAMMY CAHN
Music by JULE STYNE

With a lilt, not too fast

SECONDO

PRIMO

MERRY CHRISTMAS, DARLING

SECONDO

Words and Music by RICHARD CARPENTER
and FRANK POOLER

With expression

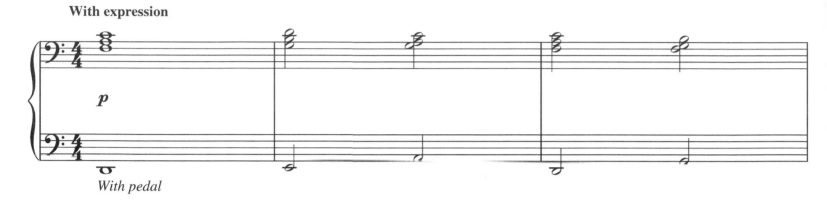

p

With pedal

Moderately slow

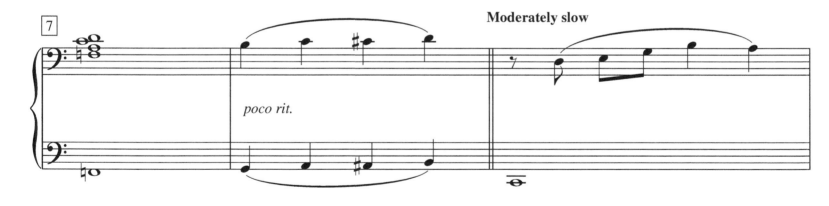

poco rit.

MERRY CHRISTMAS, DARLING

PRIMO

Words and Music by RICHARD CARPENTER
and FRANK POOLER

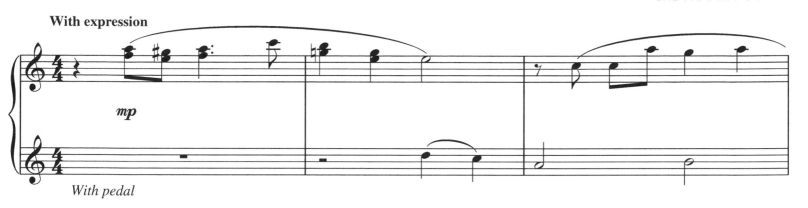

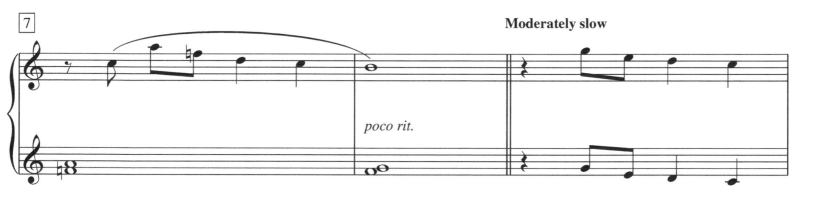

SECONDO

PRIMO

SECONDO

PRIMO

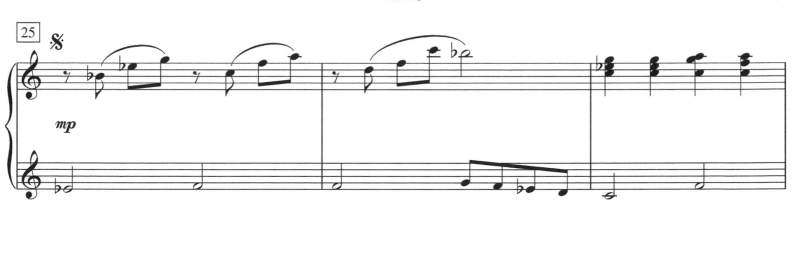

SECONDO

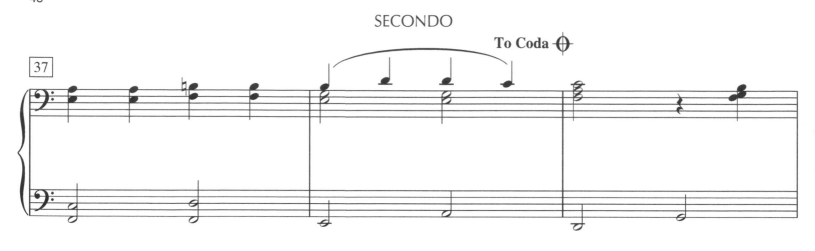

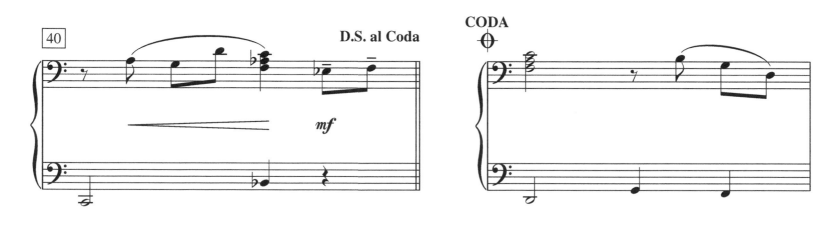

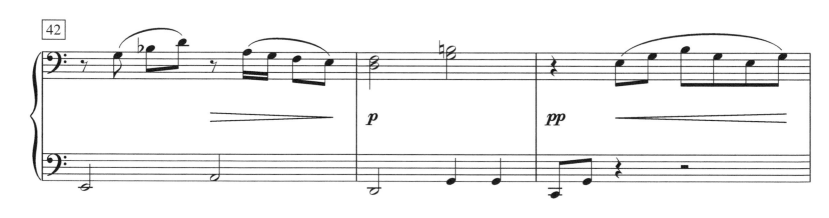

ROCKIN' AROUND THE CHRISTMAS TREE

SECONDO

Music and Lyrics by
JOHNNY MARKS

ROCKIN' AROUND
THE CHRISTMAS TREE

PRIMO

Music and Lyrics by
JOHNNY MARKS

SECONDO

PRIMO

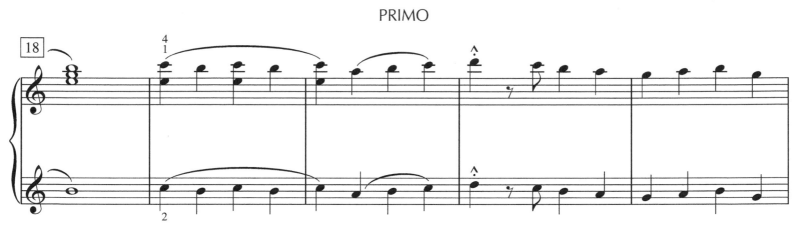

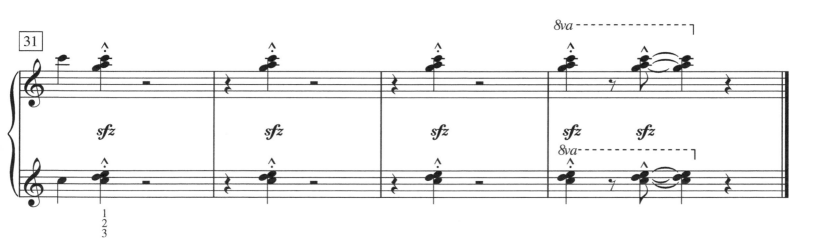

RUDOLPH THE RED-NOSED REINDEER

SECONDO

Music and Lyrics by
JOHNNY MARKS

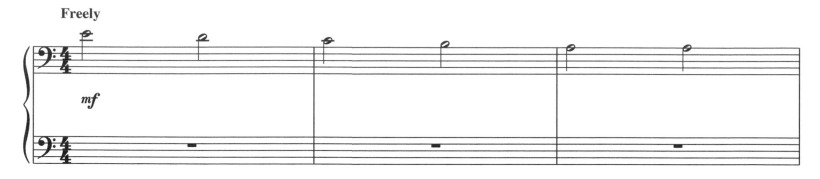

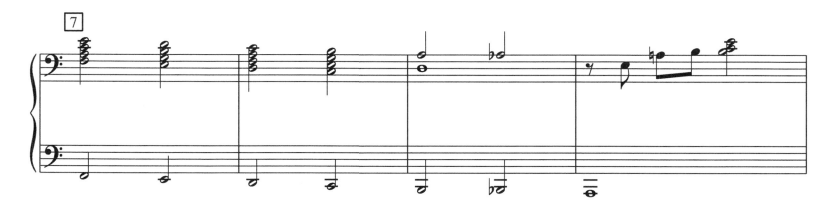

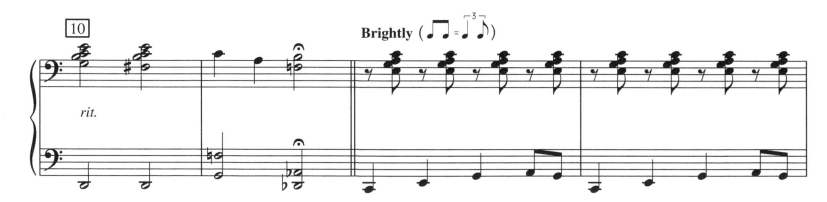

RUDOLPH THE RED-NOSED REINDEER

PRIMO

Music and Lyrics by
JOHNNY MARKS

SECONDO

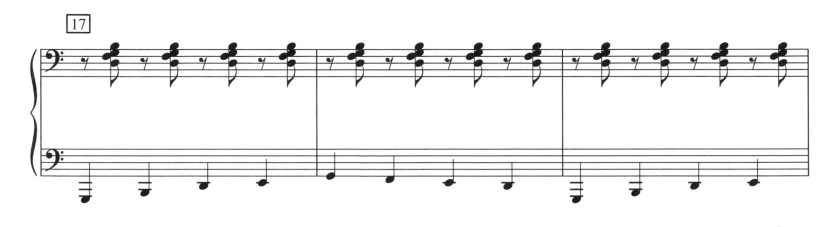

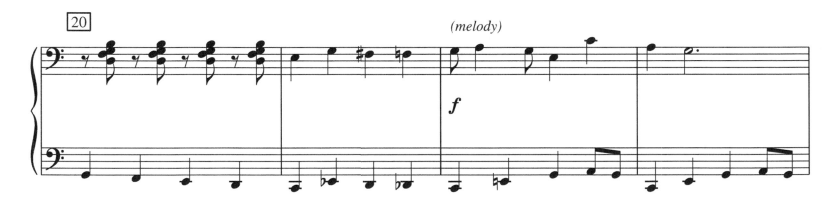

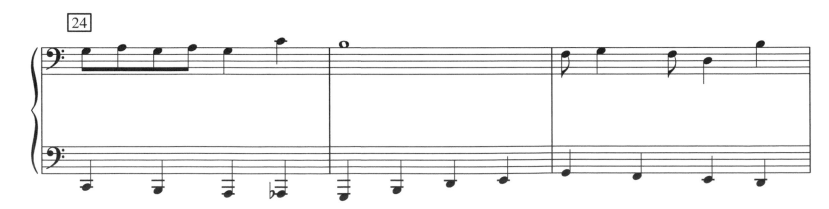

PRIMO

SECONDO

PRIMO

SECONDO

PRIMO

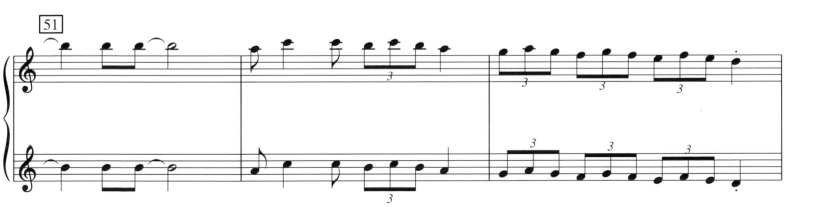

SECONDO

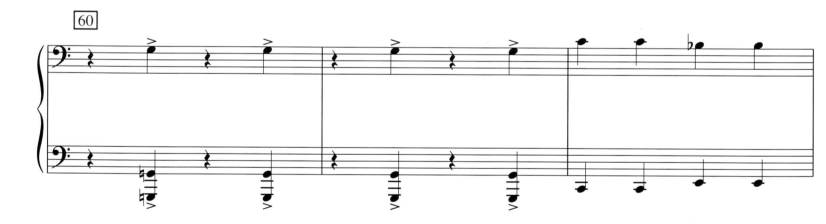

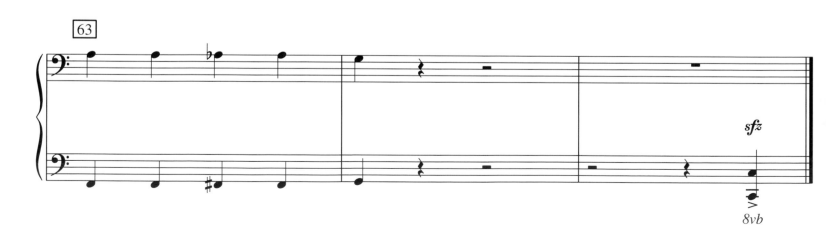

PRIMO

Piano for Two
A VARIETY OF PIANO DUETS FROM HAL LEONARD

ADELE FOR PIANO DUET

Eight of Adele's biggest hits arranged especially for intermediate piano duet! Featuring: Chasing Pavements • Hello • Make You Feel My Love • Rolling in the Deep • Set Fire to the Rain • Skyfall • Someone Like You • When We Were Young.

00172162.. $14.99

CONTEMPORARY DISNEY DUETS

8 Disney piano duets to play and perform with a friend! Includes: Almost There • He's a Pirate • I See the Light • Let It Go • Married Life • That's How You Know • Touch the Sky • We Belong Together.

00128259 .... $12.99

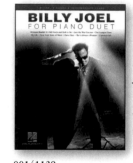

BILLY JOEL FOR PIANO DUET

Includes 8 of the Piano Man's greatest hits. Perfect as recital encores, or just for fun! Titles: Just the Way You Are • The Longest Time • My Life • Piano Man • She's Always a Woman • Uptown Girl • and more.

00141139 .... $14.99

THE BEATLES PIANO DUETS – 2ND EDITION

Features 8 arrangements: Can't Buy Me Love • Eleanor Rigby • Hey Jude • Let It Be • Penny Lane • Something • When I'm Sixty-Four • Yesterday.

00290496.. $15.99

EASY CLASSICAL DUETS

7 great piano duets to perform at a recital, play-for-fun, or sightread! Titles: By the Beautiful Blue Danube (Strauss) • Eine kleine Nachtmusik (Mozart) • Sleeping Beauty Waltz (Tchaikovsky) • and more.

00145767 Book/Online Audio $10.99

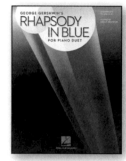

RHAPSODY IN BLUE FOR PIANO DUET

George Gershwin
Arranged by Brent Edstrom
This intimate adaptation delivers access to advancing pianists and provides an exciting musical collaboration and adventure!

00125150 .... $12.99

CHART HITS FOR EASY DUET

10 great early intermediate pop duets! Play with a friend or with the online audio: All of Me • Grenade • Happy • Hello • Just Give Me a Reason • Roar • Shake It Off • Stay • Stay with Me • Thinking Out Loud.

00159796 Book/Online Audio $12.99

THE SOUND OF MUSIC

9 arrangements from the movie/musical, including: Do-Re-Mi • Edelweiss • Maria • My Favorite Things • So Long, Farewell • The Sound of Music • and more.

00290389.. $14.99

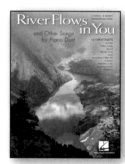

RIVER FLOWS IN YOU AND OTHER SONGS ARRANGED FOR PIANO DUET

10 great songs arranged for 1 piano, 4 hands, including the title song and: All of Me (Piano Guys) • Bella's Lullaby • Beyond • Chariots of Fire • Dawn • Forrest Gump - Main Title (Feather Theme) • Primavera • Somewhere in Time • Watermark.

00141055 .... $12.99

STAR WARS

8 intergalactic arrangements of *Star Wars* themes for late intermediate to early advanced piano duet, including: Across the Stars • Cantina Band • Duel of the Fates • The Imperial March (Darth Vader's Theme) • Princess Leia's Theme • Star Wars (Main Theme) • The Throne Room (And End Title) • Yoda's Theme.

00119405... $14.99

HAL LEONARD PIANO DUET PLAY-ALONG SERIES

This great series comes with audio that features separate tracks for the Primo and Secondo parts – perfect for practice and performance! Visit www.halleonard.com for a complete list of titles in the series!

COLDPLAY

Clocks • Paradise • The Scientist • A Sky Full of Stars • Speed of Sound • Trouble • Viva La Vida • Yellow.
00141054.. $14.99

FROZEN

Do You Want to Build a Snowman? • Fixer Upper • For the First Time in Forever • In Summer • Let It Go • Love Is an Open Door • Reindeer(s) Are Better Than People.
00128260.. $14.99

JAZZ STANDARDS

All the Things You Are • Bewitched • Cheek to Cheek • Don't Get Around Much Anymore • Georgia on My Mind • In the Mood • It's Only a Paper Moon • Satin Doll • The Way You Look Tonight.
00290577.. $14.99